ALPACA MAGIC

Stories from Longmuir Croft

by

Fiona E. Wallace

Illustrated by W.T.J. Burton

© Fiona Wallace 2005
Alpaca Magic
ISBN 0-9551787-0-3

Published by:
Alpacaknit Publications
13 St Andrews Drive
Uphall
West Lothian
EH52 6BX

Design & production co-ordinated by:
The *Better Book* Company Ltd
Havant
Hampshire
PO9 2XH

Printed in England

Contents

I dedicate this book to my
lovely granddaughter, Heather, who has a passion for
animals just like her Scottish Grandmother.

Acknowledgements

Special thanks to Bill Burton, who painted his magic throughout my book with wonderful and enchanting illustrations.

Also to Tricia Buchanan, who travelled the magical path with me, and whose brilliant guidance and editing made all the difference.

Thank you Pat Bentley for introducing me to the 'wonderful world of Alpacas', and for your continued support and friendship.

I wish to record my thanks to John Kerr(Jnr), the farmer, who on occasion rescues me from 'crisis'!

Thanks to the team of vets, Mackie & Brechin, Kirkliston, especially Dave and Iain, who rose to the challenge of looking after a new breed of animal to their practice.

Many thanks also to Richard Hartley of Alpaca Collection, who so kindly allowed me to browse through his material on Alpacas in South America.

West Lothian Ranger, Hugh Ilgunas, helped me considerably with the birds in the Bathgate Hills, and I am extremely grateful to him for his time.

The illustrations in the book were painted from photographs taken by the following:

Photographs by Murrie Thomson, Broxburn - Front & Back Cover, Page 21, 23, and 40.

Carol Mabon, Mid Calder - Page 1.

Hamish Campbell, South Queensferry (Photographer) Pages 3, 4, 6, 12, 14, 18, 24 and 29.

Scottish Farmer (John Fraser) Page 3.

Claire Millar, Uphall - Page 9.

Iain Burnside, Uphall Station - Page 19.

Gordon McBrearty, Uphall (Photographer) Page 30.

Thank you all for allowing me to use your photographs for my book.

And last, but not least, my grateful thanks to my lovely husband, Stephen, my 'dreamcatcher' in so many wonderful ways!

Introduction

LONGMUIR is a nine acre croft in West Lothian, Scotland, home to eleven alpacas, two llamas and twelve Perthshire Blackface sheep. It is sheltered on three sides by trees, with a stone dyke bordering the back, where the farm track leads up a gentle slope to the steading.

In winter, the hardwoods stand lacy and bare, while fir trees reach proudly into low, misty skies.

Bare fields make it difficult to imagine they could ever again be carpeted in fresh, luscious grass, but nature ensures that in spring, everything will grow again.

Weather is unpredictable at Longmuir. Its fields can be bathed in warm sunshine with the animals lying in wait for the cool of evening. Within minutes, skies can darken and echo round the hill to the sound of a spectacular thunderstorm, making the animals scamper for shelter.

Sometimes hours later, when the storm subsides, they emerge from their refuge to the sweet smell of the countryside, fresh and clean, with birdsong filling the air again.

To its owner, Fiona Wallace, it is a magical place - her little parcel of paradise.

As you turn the pages, the fun and adventure of Longmuir will unfold.

New beginnings

Pinkie

W.T.J.Burton.

Pinkie and Hamish

Pinkie and Hamish arrived at Longmuir one spring day, on April 3, 2002. Hamish was as black as coal, in contrast to Pinkie's whiteness, and they were the first alpacas to set foot on Longmuir ground. I was thrilled to have them. For all concerned, it was a brand new venture.

Two days later, we held the first Open Day at Longmuir. Forty invited friends and family came to see the rest of my new herd of alpacas arriving.

Hamish

I was so excited because I had not seen some of the animals for more than a year, due to the foot-and-mouth disease that had scourged the whole country.

Guests gathered in a specially erected blue and white marquee for a buffet to mark the occasion. After speeches to open the festivities, everyone waited in anticipation for midday, when

W. T. J. Burton

the remaining eight alpacas were due to arrive from Cumbria.

Alpacas love to travel. They are calm and do not become stressed. Once en route, they will settle and enjoy the ride. Despite this, Pinkie and Hamish were tired after their long haul from Sussex.

The two were carefully introduced to their new home. At that time, there were no paddocks and the ground was not manicured as it is today.

It was a vast, uninteresting field, unlike home. It was also a strange country, with the Scottish air much cooler than Sussex and I could feel their loneliness.

As they began to wander, all the time staying close to each other, it became clear they were unsettled. Both made a continuous humming sound, which they make when distressed.

They lay in a boggy corner of the field, which looked out on to the road. Later, I had to fence off this area because of the muddy mess they got into lying in the bog. Pinkie looked as black as Hamish!

I felt so sad for them, but I knew that soon, things would be different. They certainly were!

Midday came, the lorry with the eight alpacas arrived, and the middle gate to the croft was opened in readiness. The large lorry doors swung open and the tailgate lowered.

Within seconds, eight alpacas, black, white, and brown, bounded into the field. The herd took to the croft instantly and settled without hesitation. It was an extraordinary sight.

Guests were also in the field. They took photographs, videos and chatted excitedly among themselves. Everyone was thrilled to see alpacas for the first time. Meanwhile, in the corner, stood Pinkie and Hamish, two lonely alpacas from Sussex, watching all the activity.

Suddenly, they sprang to their feet and ran towards the eight other alpacas. Pinkie and Hamish immediately herded with their new friends and bonded within a few days. It was a beautiful moment to treasure, and I can, thanks to a guest who captured it on video.

As the weeks passed, I discovered the humming sounds from Pinkie and Hamish also served to maintain contact between the two, since they had relied so heavily on each other for comfort and security in their first two lonely days.

Open day at Longmuir

Angus

W.T.J. Burton.

4

Angus

Angus is a white alpaca. He is a friendly animal - to his own kind and to humans, but he could have many other titles - ambassador, dancer, or even pick-pocket.

When new animals arrive at Longmuir, Angus is first to greet them and say 'hello', while the rest of the herd stands back, eyeing the newcomer with some trepidation.

Although he is charming and friendly, Angus can sometimes find himself in deep trouble.

One day, as I walked down the field to the feeding trough, with a yellow bucket full of his favourite treats - camelid nuts, he came bouncing toward me. Up and down he went, until he was alongside. Then he dropped his head into the bucket.

No-one was expecting what happened next. The handle of the bucket went right over his head and down his long neck. What a shock he got!

All the other alpacas, which had been watching intently, ran away up the field in fright.

Angus danced and bounced around trying to shake off the yellow bucket, but it was so full of nuts and weighed so heavily, it would not budge. Suddenly, he stopped and stood still, trembling like a big, woolly, wobbly jelly.

I approached him slowly and quietly, talking to him softly. Although he was in a state, he allowed me to lift the bucket up his long neck and over his head to free him.

What a surprise he got when the
bucket handle slipped over his neck.

W.T.J Burton.

He stood dazed for a few seconds, then ran off to greet his friends. He missed his treats though, because after all the dancing about, most of the nuts had scattered all over the grass!

One day, Angus was in a mischievous mood while I was in the field feeding carrots to the alpacas and llamas. In the right hand pocket of my jacket, I carried the keys to the croft, but I was not aware that the decorative crystal ball of the key-ring was dangling out of my pocket.

Angus was in pick-pocket mode. He rushed over to me, pulled the crystal ball with keys attached, from my pocket between his teeth, and ran off down the field. With a clear sense of mischief, he ran round and round the field, with me in pursuit, until I was exhausted trying to catch him.

Chasing Angus was no use so I needed a plan to bring him to me. Camelid nuts - his favourite treat! Off I went to fill his bucket and returned to the field calling his name.

As soon as Angus saw the yellow bucket in my hand, he skipped over the field until he was standing right in front of me, with the keys comically dangling from his mouth.

'Hello Angus,' I said. 'Keys in exchange for nuts?' Guess what - he obliged!

Shearing time

It was June, the month when alpacas are sheared.

Angus was in the small pen with the other alpacas, watching Ben, the shearer, and his assistant as they drove into the pen and began setting up the shearing equipment. They placed a long board on the trailer, forming what looked like a large table, waist height.

Ben and his assistant expertly removed all the fleece.

Angus was proud of his new, clean-cut image.

Angus was first. The two men lifted him on to the table and tied his legs; first, the front legs together, then the back. Ben's assistant held Angus's neck to help keep him still. Ben began his work, first trimming Angus's feet.

Next, he sheared the fleece from Angus's body. Ben worked back and forth, occasionally oiling the clipping shears so they would not get too hot. He expertly removed the entire fleece, until Angus looked as if he had pulled a zip down his front and stepped out of his warm winter coat.

Finally, Angus had his teeth checked to make sure all was well.

I gathered up the fleece. First, I put the 'blanket' wool, from the main part of the body, into hessian sacks. Next, the 'skirting' from the legs and neck, was put into separate sacks, to hang in the shed.

Angus's top knot was gently trimmed with scissors, but not too short, because it helps to keep flies from his eyes.

Looking as if he had just had a 'shampoo and set' at the hairdresser's, Angus proudly strutted towards the rest of the herd, as if to say; 'Look chaps, it's not so bad after all.'

Before long, the whole job was finished and the rest of the herd was sheared. Sleep came quickly to all the alpacas that evening and they were soon snoozing contentedly in their paddock.

Meanwhile, a long ladder was raised to the roof of the shed, and once all the hessian sacks were filled with alpaca fleece they were swung from the rafters, ready to be sent away.

All the fleece was packed into
hessian sacks and hung from
the rafters in the shed.

Fred

Fred & Brucie

More than a year ago, I bought two llamas - Fred and Brucie. When they arrived at Longmuir everything seemed calm.

Three days after their arrival, disruption had broken out in the herd. The peace that had once reigned at Longmuir Croft was gone. Now there was unhappiness.

Fred was so naughty, breaking fences and fighting constantly with Brucie, that I had to make a special pen for him. Meanwhile, Brucie herded with the alpacas.

It soon became clear that Fred was not really the naughty one. It was Brucie. He fell out with two of the alpacas and had to go into a paddock on his own.

'Dear me,' I thought. 'What have I done?'

What could I do to bring them all together and to make peace with each other? It was a difficult problem, but I had a plan.

First, I made sure, that Fred and Brucie could see one another, I had discovered quite early on, that if they could not make eye contact, they became restless.

Each day, I fed them their favourite camelid nuts. Brucie always ate his with relish. Fred refused.

It took several weeks before Fred gave way to the bucket of nuts. From that day on, he became more confident, made eye contact easily, and was not frightened when I approached him in his pen.

Within a few months, I was able to herd him with the alpacas.

Happiness reigned again. Fred would rush around the field, jump joyfully in the air, make circles, and roll on the ground over and over again.

For Fred, life seemed not so bad after all, but there was still poor Brucie to make happy. It took another seven-and-a-half months before Brucie could join Fred and the alpacas, and herd together as one big happy family.

Constant love and care helped Brucie bond with his friends. To see them now, no-one could imagine they had ever been anything but the best of friends.

Brucie

Fred

Fred is handsome, appealing, well-mannered, and very much a gentleman. He is russet in colour, has huge brown eyes, with the longest eyelashes, and gorgeous, banana-shaped ears.

He settled quickly at Longmuir and soon became champion of the alpacas. He stood much taller than Brucie, so he assumed leadership of the herd. Even Brucie willingly came under his guidance.

Despite his status, Fred would stand back if any alpacas approached his eating area.

In many other ways, Fred became a tower of strength and I came to rely on him for special jobs on the croft.

At lambing time in April, when a lamb or twins were born, the sound of their bleating carried to the far end of the field. Within seconds, Fred would rush to the maternity pen, to see that all was well.

With his head over the fence, he would gaze at the new-born lambs with such softness in his eyes, he endeared himself to everyone who was watching.

By the time seventeen lambs had been born, Fred was exhausted, but he continued his patrol of the pen on three sides, ensuring the lambs were safe and well. The ewes and lambs showed no fear of him, and were quite settled in his presence.

When it was time for the lambs to leave the maternity pen with

Fred chased the fox right out of the field

their mothers to graze the bottom field, Fred and the alpacas patrolled the top field, keeping a watchful eye on the flock.

Lambing time also brought the threat of foxes coming into the field. Alpacas and llamas do not like foxes, or dogs that look like them. If a fox is in sight, they will tightly pack themselves together and send out a piercing warning cry.

On one such occasion, Fred could be seen chasing a dog fox across the top field until it bounded over the stone dyke wall, disappearing into the forest.

Fred's devotion to the lambs never wavered. He was especially fond of the first-born lamb. It would stand on a square bale at the side of the fence to allow Fred to lean over and lick its face. The lamb would just stand there, enjoying the attention.

He is the tallest of them all, but Fred is a giant in many ways!

The new-born lamb just stood there,
enjoying the attention.

Magic

Of all the alpacas at Longmuir, Magic has the longest neck. He easily stands above the rest of the herd.

He is mostly black in colour, with white under his chin and splotches of white all down his neck.

Magic has an aloof, superior look. When he first came to the croft, I would bow to him and say: 'Good morning, your Majesty.'

He would look down his nose at me and I wondered what on earth he was thinking.

Gradually, it became clear that this was a special and most wise alpaca. He took everything in his stride, paced himself, never hurrying over anything. He ate with relish, and did not fight with his friends. In fact, he was a good all-rounder.

Once I got to know him, 'Your Majesty' seemed an unsuitable name, so I changed it to 'Magic', because that is exactly what he was.

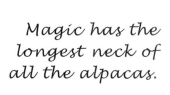

Magic has the longest neck of all the alpacas.

One of his favourite pastimes is rolling on the ground, twisting himself, this way and that. Another of his greatest pleasures is to sunbathe, which all alpacas enjoy.

He would lie contentedly in the sun, with his neck stretched out on the grass. If you listened carefully, you could hear him snoring quietly, seeming to have the most wonderful dreams.

You can almost hear a sigh of contentment as Magic cools his feet.

Being among Alpacas is therapeutic. Having owned them for a few years, I have never lost the feeling of well being while in their company.

Every animal in the herd expresses its individuality and there is something uniquely special to each one. For Magic, it is to stand in the water trough and wash his feet. The first time I saw him do this, I wondered what he could be up to, but I became quite used to him.

On warm days, he could be seen strolling up to the big water trough at the shed, and gently lifting his feet into the water. He would splash about, then try to lower himself in, to enjoy the coolness of the water even more.

Alpacas are truly herding animals - they do everything together. Once the other alpacas saw Magic cooling himself at the water trough, they began to follow suit. It seemed I had the cleanest alpacas in Scotland!

The only downside to this experience was that the water troughs are actually filled with the alpacas' drinking water. Now, they have to be cleaned regularly, all because of Magic and his magical ways.

Bute

When I first set eyes on this fawn alpaca, it was love at first sight. I thought: 'Isn't he a beauty!' That is how he got his name - Bute.

He was a retired stud male from Cumbria and when he came to the croft in December, nearly two years ago, he immediately took leadership of the other alpacas.

There was never a murmur of dissent from the other animals,

Bute brought a wonderful gift to the croft.

W.T.J.Burton,

just a quiet acceptance that this was the leader for them. From that day, the herd never looked back.

Bute was a natural 'look-out'. He would spend much of his time watching everything that was going on. Even a tiny speck moving in the distance would have his full attention, until he was sure it bore no threat to him or his herd.

Until Bute arrived, I had never seen any of my alpacas 'stott'. To see him 'stotting' in the snow was a wonderful sight

Stotting is when an alpaca thrusts his body upward and forward, landing on all four feet at the same time, with a stiff-legged stance. It reminds me of the horses on a merry-go-round at a fair, all going up and down.

Bute displayed such energy in the field. He was like lightning - here, there and everywhere. The other alpacas would follow him at speed, at the same time performing fantastic dancing steps and twirls in the air between stotting, I would hold my breath, wondering if they would land on the ground in one piece. They always did.

I read that when llamas and alpacas 'stott' it is a sign of great happiness and health.

What a wonderful gift Bute brought to Longmuir.

Bute leads the alpacas through the snow

Spats

Spats was the first alpaca I bought and first of eleven in the Longmuir herd.

He was black and white. When I first saw him, I fell in love with his huge, sensitive, deep brown eyes, and his clown-like appearance.

Spats seemed the perfect name because of his black and white feet, which looked like the shoes and spats worn by an old-fashioned gentleman. Visiting family and friends always pointed him out as their favourite.

W.T.J.Burton.

Spats

Despite his popularity, he was very shy and sought security by hiding behind the other alpacas. Smaller and not as bulky as the others, Spats was always at the bottom end of the pecking order and I had to keep an eye on him to make sure he ate his ration of nuts.

Alpacas are fastidious in their toilet habits. They are so houseproud that they dung in the same area, not all over the field, like sheep or cattle. When they move to a new area to dung, they will not graze the used area for more than two years.

Spats is funny when he joins the others at the alpaca 'latrine'.

24

He positions himself carefully, stretching out his back legs so far, he almost does the splits, like a ballerina. I thought he might split himself in half, and I often 'split my sides' with laughter watching him.

When the alpacas stop grazing at their latrine, it is easy to imagine how high the grass would grow, so the tractor is brought out to keep the area short and tidy. If not, the field would look like a patchwork maze of long and short grasses!

Spats has special ways of dealing with flies, especially in June, July and August, when they bother him most. His antics are hilarious. He can contort himself into comical scratching positions that have to be seen to be believed. He is the undoubted comedian of the herd.

Spats clown-like appearance reflects in his antics

The Mystery of the Disappearing Fleece

In summer, just after the alpacas have been shorn, little tufts of fleece can be seen lying around on the ground.

One year, as I worked my daily routine around the alpaca pen, I noticed the pieces of fleece were beginning to disappear. Where were they going? Who or what was taking them - and why?

At first, it seemed birds could be the culprits, taking fleece to line their nests, but I had seen no birds near the alpaca pens. It was also unlikely birds would be nest-building in the middle of summer.

One day, while I was putting straw on the floor of the alpaca shelter, something caught my eye in the far corner. Curiosity took over and I went to investigate. There in the corner was a large pile of the alpaca fleece that had been disappearing.

A closer look revealed the fleece was moving up and down. We certainly had a visitor to our croft, but what was it?

The temptation to look underneath was overwhelming, but I did not want to disturb this cosy little nest, in case mother smelled an intruder and would not return to look after her young. Having guessed it was rabbits, I left them to it.

On mentioning the incident to a farm-hand, he immediately replied it could be rats. It was an appalling suggestion. Rats were unwanted visitors to the croft, because they can carry disease, but he said he wanted to make sure.

We went to the alpaca shelter for a proper look. The farmhand gently parted the alpaca fleece and we were astonished at what we found. Buried deep in the warm alpaca fleece lay four leverets, baby hares.

They were the smallest, cutest baby animals I have ever seen, with ears almost as big as they were. With a rush of maternal instinct, I knew these vulnerable little creatures had to be protected from foxes that patrolled the stone wall at the back of the croft.

There was no need to worry. I was not the only one wanting to protect this family of baby hares, the alpacas did too - and they were making a splendid job of it. Why had I not noticed?

On rainy days, when the alpacas stood in their shelter, they never ventured near that corner. Instead, they grouped themselves to one side, which was unusual for them.

Alpacas always amaze me with their wisdom. They already knew about the little visitors and had been protecting them from outside danger all along.

As the baby hares grew, they could be seen bobbing in and out of the shelter, playing games together and having lots of fun.

I became apprehensive at this stage, because we live in buzzard country. One swoop was all it would take for a bird of prey to carry off the precious baby hares.

Between the alpacas, myself and of course, mother hare, four beautiful leverets were safely reared, to everyone's delight. I felt so privileged to have been part of it.

Buried deep in the warm alpaca fleece
lay four leverets, baby hares.

Snowflake & Bonzo Question time

Now that you have met almost all the residents at Longmuir, you will agree that alpacas are fascinating animals. In this final chapter, an imaginary interview has been created with Snowflake and Bonzo. In it, there are interesting details about the characteristics of these friendly creatures - straight from the alpacas' mouth!

Q: It is obvious how you got your name, isn't it.

Snowflake: Yes, I have a white patch right on top of my nose that looks as if a snowflake has fallen on it

Q: Bonzo. How did you get your name.

Bonzo: I don't really know. I think my owner just pulled it out of a hat.

Q: Would you mind answering a few questions about yourselves.

Snowflake

W.T.J.Burton.

Snowflake and **Bonzo:** Okay. Fire away.

Q: Where do you originally come from?

Bonzo: That's easy. South America. It could be Peru or Bolivia.

Snowflake (not wanting to be outdone): Chile and Argentina too.

Q: People often ask this question. Do alpacas spit at human beings.

Snowflake and Bonzo thought for a few seconds.

Bonzo (dryly)**:** This behaviour is reserved for alpacas, not people.

Bonzo

Their ears were twitching. It was clearly a sensitive subject, better not taken any further.

Q: When you spit, it smells awful. Why is that.

Snowflake: Well, it would. After all, it is chewed grass. What do you expect.

Q: Is it true that you hum.

Bonzo: That's not a very nice thing to say.

Q: I mean humming, as in making humming sounds, being vocal.

Bonzo: Yes, we do that sort of humming. We hum if we are upset or lonely, or if for any reason, our owner separates us from the herd. Sometimes we hum just as a bonding sound.

Q: Are you intelligent.

Snowflake and Bonzo are silent.

Snowflake: We think so, of course. We are extremely inquisitive and we learn very quickly.

Q: How long do you live.

Snowflake and Bonzo, together: For around 20 years.

Q: Do you bite.

Snowflake: Humph! I don't think much of that question. What do you think, Bonzo.

Bonzo (with his nose in the air): Personally, I think we are very loveable. So the answer is no, we don't bite.

Q: (trying hard not to offend them): What kinds of ways do you communicate with each other.

Bonzo: You mean, you have never noticed? It is obvious, you know. We are doing it right now. Can you not guess?

Q: With your ears, tail and head.

Bonzo: It is subtler than that. We can change our ear positions to show alertness, happiness or displeasure.

Silly really, to ask if they were intelligent. Quickly moving on.

Q: What do you eat.

Snowflake (as Bonzo chewed his cud): We are grazers and browsers, doing well on most types of pastures. In winter, our owner supplements our feeding with soft, meadow hay and nuts.

Q: Are you really related to llamas.

Bonzo (finished chewing): Yes, we are.

Q: What differences are there between you.

Snowflake: Gosh. Have to think about that one. Let me see... For a start, llamas are bigger than we are. Of course, their fleece is not as good as ours is. We have a beautiful soft fibre. If I remember correctly, llamas have a double coat, with coarse guard hairs on top, and short softer fibres underneath.

Q: Is there anything else you would like to tell me about yourselves.

Snowflake and Bonzo go into deep thought.

Bonzo: We thought you might have asked us different types of questions.

Q: Such as.

Snowflake: Did you know there are two types of alpacas.

No.

Bonzo: Ha! Got you there. There are two types of alpacas, Suri and Huacaya. Snowflake and I are Huacaya, and proud of it too.

Snowflake: Do you know what a baby alpaca is called.

A cub?

Snowflake and **Bonzo** together: No, no, no. It is called a 'cria'.

How could anyone dare to say alpacas are not intelligent.

Thanks to Snowflake and Bonzo for adding this insight to our story of the residents at Longmuir Croft.

Country Birds around Longmuir

Brown Buzzard

Buzzards

LONGMUIR lies within beautiful countryside, to the east of the Bathgate Hills, West Lothian, Scotland, with the hills rising to just over 1000ft (304.8 metres) at Cairnpapple. The landscape provides lochs and burns, hills and farmland, woods and dykes, marshes and grassland.

With this rich and varied habitat, it is a haven for many birds. More than 120 species of birds are recorded for the Bathgate Hills. Breeding birds of prey seen in the area include sparrow hawks, kestrels, tawny owls, merlins and buzzards.

Once, I watched in wonder a flock of swans landing gracefully in my fields and on another occasion, I was honoured by a carpet of curlews, so many that I could not count them all.

Buzzards were rare in West Lothian 15 years ago, but now they are flourishing. Almost every day I see one perched on a straining post and I often hear the high-pitched 'mewing' or 'pee-yooing' sound of its voice.

It is a fairly large bird, with plumage from pale to dark brown in colour and a white patch under the wings. Buzzards live in woods and scattered woodland with their territory spreading into lowland farming areas, where they hunt for rabbits, mice, voles and small birds to eat

Its nest is a large, bulky structure, made of sticks, usually built high in conifers or pines. The female lays 2-3 eggs in April-May.

Sometimes, when I am working in the field with the alpacas, a buzzard will startle me, swooping down so close that I can see him carrying his prey in his talons. He is so quick, that I can never identify what he has caught and before I can catch my breath he has soared high into the sky.

Magpies

MAGPIES are daily visitors to the fields.

While the alpacas and llamas are feeding at the troughs, magpies hop and dance on and around the nearby fences waiting for the animals to finish. On really cold mornings when they are eager to feed, you can hear their harsh chattering as if to say: 'Hurry up, we are hungry.'

As soon as the last alpaca finishes feeding and leaves the pen, the magpies swoop into the feeding troughs looking for leftovers.

They also love to explore the red plastic tubs filled with high energy sheep lick for the blackface ewes. Keeping balance with their long black tails, they perch on the boxes, digging their beaks deep into the contents.

Magpies are intelligent birds and are easily recognised with their unmistakable black and white plumage, long tails and comical hop-skip-hop walk. Close up and in sunshine, their black feathers give off a distinctive purplish-blue iridescent sheen.

The Magpies love to explore the red plastic tubs

History of the Alpaca

CAMELIDS, animals belonging to the family of camels and llamas, were domesticated thousands of years ago by Native American peoples in the Andean Highlands of South America. While they kept llamas and alpacas, the alpacas were bred primarily for their fibre.

Alpaca fibre was first recorded in the Chavin civilization (850-200BC) where it played an important role in religious textiles. Light in weight and large, these textiles helped communication among a culturally diverse and illiterate population. Alpaca fibre also became a valuable export to these herders.

The Paracas, an early coastal people (200BC-AD200), practised irrigation, agriculture and lived in villages. They also had copious supplies of alpaca fibre and they appreciated its warmth, softness and glossy sheen.

In richly dyed colours and intricate designs, usually combined with cotton, alpaca fibre was used to make burial coverings, which were among the most spectacular in Peru.

The use of alpaca fibre spread throughout Peru and reached its peak in the Inca Empire from the mid 1400 to 1500s.

Cloistered noblewomen wove alpaca cloth into symbolic gifts for coming of age, marriage and funerals. Many patterns were simple and plain, coloured garments were used to indicate status and occupation.

In 1536, the Spanish conquest of the Incas brought European

designs and new weaving looms, which in turn gave new meaning and value to the cloth. Many traditional methods of weaving and use of colour and pattern remain today in Native communities.

Alpacas in Britain

Industrialist Sir Titus Salt, was the first to spin alpaca into yarn in Britain in 1836. From a sheep farming background, he had moved to Bradford to learn the wool manufacturing trade.

While training, he discovered some discarded bales of unknown fibre in the Bradford Wool Exchange. They had arrived as ballast in ships from Peru. He realised the long, silky alpaca fibres could produce a beautiful, lustrous worsted yarn and cloth.

In so doing, Titus Salt began the biggest and most successful alpaca worsted cloth business in the world, selling not only throughout Britain, but also in Western Europe, North America and Japan.

In the 19th century, he was commissioned to make crinolines and coats from alpaca fibre, for Queen Victoria, a leader of fashion in her time. Wearing an alpaca overcoat, Her Majesty was pictured viewing her own herd of alpacas in Windsor Great Park with her consort, Prince Albert.

Manufacturing garments from alpaca was further boosted in the 20th century, when two mills, Mitchell and Company, and Inca Group, developed the spinning industry in Peru and the exportation of raw, white fibre.

In February 1974, Pat Bentley was to become a significant influence of alpaca keeping in the UK.

While on holiday in Peru, she visited the grassy slopes of Cuzco. There she touched an alpaca for the first time and was spellbound by its captivating brown eyes, gentleness and the feel of its fleece. She vowed one day she would breed alpacas.

In 1982, she bought two young males from Northamptonshire. They were followed by three females, two from Holland and one from what was then East Germany. It was the start of a pioneering path on which she learned to nurture and care for these animals.

Pat realised that more alpacas were needed because she believed they could have a long-term future in this country.

In 1992, a licence was issued from the British Government to import alpacas from Chile into the UK. This was followed by the first two importations of alpacas in 1996 and 1997.

Some of these animals went to Pat at her Cumbrian home and they were valuable in improving her stock.

Today, there are over 600 alpaca owners in the UK, with a national herd of about 12 to 15,000 animals. Most are in England, with smaller herds in Scotland, Wales and Ireland. Due to the variety of colours of alpacas, the numbers still fall short of producing a viable fibre business in the UK, but each year that goal becomes closer.

More than 20 years ago, alpacas were virtually unknown in the UK. Today, they are a beautiful and permanent feature of the British countryside.

Fleece Facts

Alpacas have beautiful fleece, but some are better quality than others, because they are less coarse.

Currently, in the United Kingdom, the national herd numbers approximately 12 to 15,000 alpacas, producing beautiful, high quality fibre. One alpaca can produce 3kg of fleece per year.

The fibre is warm, light and very soft. It feels like silk to the touch. Clothing made from alpaca fibre is thermal and water resistant.

Unlike sheep, alpaca fibre is not greasy. Sheep are protected from the rain by lanolin in their fleece, so rain cannot penetrate. With no lanolin, the alpaca becomes soaked to the skin. It is easy to understand why alpacas do not like rain and will usually seek shelter.

Alpacas come in a wide range of natural colours. They can be pure white, through to shades of fawn and dark browns. Especially beautiful are hues of rose, blue-grey and jet black.

Devoid of natural grease, alpaca fleece is a pleasure for hand spinners to work with. When the alpacas are shorn, the 'clip' is sent to England, where it is sorted and graded, according to its fineness, staining, or whether there is debris stuck in it.

The finest fleece comes from the 'blanket' or 'saddle' on the animals back. 'Skirting' is fibre from the belly and leg, and to the front of the chest. It is poorer quality and often contains coarse guard hairs that may itch or prickle the skin if a garment was to be made from it. However, the skirting has useful thermal qualities and can be used to make rugs and fill duvets.

The first clip from a young alpaca is known as 'baby alpaca'. It is a very fine fleece and commands a good price.

'Bye for now...